Moments Strange

Moments Strange

Poems by

Ed Block

Cover by Shay Culligan
Cover art by Ed Block

ISBN: 978-1-63980-109-1

Kelsay Books
502 South 1040 East, A-119
American Fork, Utah 84003
Kelsaybooks.com

Acknowledgments

Grateful acknowledgment goes to the following publications in which these poems first appeared.

Lake Country Journal: "Crows," "Cones In April," "Radishes in Spring," "Spring Migration"

Plainsongs: "My maiden aunts"

Nebraska Life: "Grackle," "Summer Soldier"

The World & I Online: "Widower Bald," "Spring Dandy," "A Shower in June," "Found Things"

Elm Grove News-Independent: "Flowering Crab," and "Syllabic"

Literary Matters, Online publication of the *Association of Literary Scholars, Critics, and Writers:* "Looking for Norma," "From the Air," "Peonies in Fall," "Spring Flood," and "Hotel Malawi"

Seasons of Change (Finishing Line Press, 2016)*:* "Chikale Beach," "Cinzano, White & Red," "35th and Morgan," "At an Exhibition," "Before Midnight," "Rummage Sale," "Suburban Derelict," and "Tam's Gone Dark"

Weekly Avocet: "Around the Feeder"

"Bramble, Journal of the Wisconsin Fellowship of Poets: "Dancing In Time," "Far From Home"

2020 Wisconsin Poet's Calendar: "A Bouquet"

Honorable Mention in WFOP's 2018 *Triad* competition,
    "Nature's Due"

Halfway to the North Pole (The Door County Poets Collective)
    Sturgeon Bay, WI: "A Washington Island Tale"

2020 Annual Report of the Mississippi Valley Conservancy:
    "In the Driftless"

Contents

Memories

Out of Africa and Places Near and Far

Africa

The Neighborhood

Up North, Out West

Far & Farewell

Moments Strange

Moments Strange

All life is strange
a congeries
of moments
creatures new and old
freighted with portents
meaning past
and present
what's to come

the dust deceit
the nitty-gritty everyday
and never before
a flood
of feeling
and forever
times and seasons
icy dreams
and place astrain
with overflowing
memories
of home and faraway
of moments
torn from out the fast
and growing agony

a life in large outline
that fines itself down
to the smallest
moments strange,
but each astonishing
and tugging at the line
of high or deep
desire and wholly
never always dear.

Spring and Summer

Early March

Cold and quiet on a winter morning.
Sun just up, the light lies gently
on the dying snow. Gray with yellow
highlights run from east to north,
and in the sky a last few shreds
of cloud stray out across the lake,
chased by the weather coming
from the west.
             A trail of rabbit tracks
beneath the birch is disappearing,
final evidence of last night's fête
of foraging beneath the feeder hanging there.

Syllabic

Winter let loose very slowly
this year. Mounds of dirty snow still
mark the yard. Rings of grass around
the trees grow slowly as the sun
appears infrequently, while buds
on trees and bushes hesitate
to grow, the branches looking, still,
like finger bones raised to the sky.

Spring Migration

for Ted Kooser

The snow around the tree recedes.
Their winter trails exposed, the voles
make for the matted leaves, the cracks
between the lannon stone,
the gaps beneath the bent and broken iris stems
that mark the garden's edge. They
curse the march of spring and vow
to stay abed all day, when once
they find their summer home again.

Cones in April

Pinecones, grain-ripe, resin-rich,
a bucketful beneath the trees.
Atop the forty feet
of evergreen more cluster,
hang pendant,
waiting for a wind.
Resiny cobs, a bucketful,
gathered like windfall apples—
but on a sunswept April day.

Sprinkle in a fallen bough,
green needles;
a still-life for an afternoon.
Profligate proliferation of
seed pods, wind-heaved,
waste of nature,
ever-fertile, scattered on the lawn,
they fill the pail and mind
with thoughts of spring.

Spring Flood

After Aldo Leopold

In the rows
now flooded by the river,
carp swim happily.

They wriggle through
the drowned cornstalks,
rubbing scaly sides
against the green,
and whisper to each other.

Spring explorers, these,
they kiss the mud
with baby mouths.

But, interlopers, they churn
up the water, finding
leaves and cobs left

from the fall. Till water
recedes, carp frolic
in forbidden territories,
making fun
of patient farmers' plows.

In Spring

As I prowl about the yard
and watch for signs that life
is coming back to ground
and garden, trees and bushes
that have suffered cold for more
months than I want to count,
I see the crocus, purple in the grass,
the first leaves of the primrose
in the flowerbed; the hyacinth,
delphinium and jonquil all
beginning to rejoice the coming spring.
These iambic lines, self-soothing
like the tunes I hum, are my defense
against temptations to be glum.

Bridal Wreath

Some fourteen years I've watched you,
season in and season out,
marking the corner of our yard.
In fall and winter, non-descript—
a cloud of dusky branches, bending
to the lawn. Come April, mowing
the grass, I nearly stumbled into you,
like Moses at the burning bush:
a milk-white apparition
defying sense and understanding.

Bridal wreath, or bride's bouquet,
too delicate to hold.
In bud, like tiny fireworks,
star cluster, Roman candle
set to burst. Then, fully bloomed,
as quick as fireworks to scatter
brightness, petals on the grass.
A white cascade spills over
a fountain with its jets of foam
pours out upon the lawn.

Familiar, yet so new, and *other;*
radiant, the driven blossoms
icy white, yet delicate;
the bush festoons the lawn.
It's like an anniversary:
the late-May blooming of the bridal wreath.

The bridal wreath speaks richness,
purity, and love; creation,
fertile, generous, flaunting
its festiveness;

profusion, preciousness;
its necklaces of blossom, pendants;
bangles for a bride.

Now unearthly radiant white
has paled to antique bone,
then golden age. The petals
fall like drops of white;
in clouds of white descend—
covering the grass like fallen snow.
In autumn, bridal wreath is rust and gold.

Around the Feeder

The feeder on the window
draws a motley chord of birds.

The evergreen is full of voices
speaking alien, avian words.

Chickadees are scolding
from the branches of the birch,

and finches fight and shoulder
one another from the perch.

Sparrows, from the feeder,
drop like leaves upon the ground

to rummage in the seed pods
that are scattered all around.

Radishes in Spring

Radishes, with long
white roots,
like mouse tails,
lie huddled
in the kitchen bowl.

Their bright alarm
shrieks out of May,
green leaves,
and gardens;
sun, and dark warm soil.

Flowering Crab

The crab tree,
fully bloomed a day,
already drops
its blossoms. Petals
carried by the wind,
they scatter
like our later dreams
of summer joy,
before that season's
even here.

Spring Dandy

The robin, most erect of birds;
its yellow beak expresses
pride, disdain, or pique;
but also character, panache.
Its orange waistcoat,
ostentation, self-importance,
a veritable Cyrano of birds;
the only dandy of the spring.

Grackle

The grackle,
gentle charlatan,
black morning-coat
gone green from age—

its tails mismatched—
steps unobtrusively
through unmowed grass,
a shabby vagrant of the spring,

and searches with stiletto beak
for things left out
or dropped, or lost.

Summer Soldier

The redwing blackbird,
military bird, complete with epaulettes;
he strides upon his watch,
a power wire, his neat
black uniform with round-cut tail;
then dives, with trill,
into the backyard hedge,
to flush a fellow redwing out.

A Shower in June

Each rain drop taps
a leaf.

Each leaf awakes
to shake itself.

Then rain comes on,
and every tree

is live in momentary motion.
After rain, the birds are quieter.

Drops from the eaves
fall, one by one, into the blackened wooden tub.

The sky is gray,
the air is cool.

A grackle sits
upon a log

that marks an old tree's passing.
A breeze awakens in the fresh June air.

Evening on the Porch

Sitting, listening to the rain increase
from drizzle to soft showers;
drops increasing in the bucket
at the corner of the gutter. Sit
and breathe in peace before you turn
to other pages, other duties.

Now the drops become a rhythm
in the bucket, heartbeats, speeded up;
the rain is running. The drops
are now a runner's heartbeat,
strong and steady; in the lead,
and feeling confident.

Now the air is cool, the breeze has dropped;
the rain has stopped. The drops are slowing.
Now the race is at an end;
the runner pauses, ribbon broken; the pulse
slows down. A steady thump,
thump, thump, within the breast of night.

Sitting at Night in My Basement Office

The mouse behind the wall
is quiet; birdseed, stolen,
in its cheeks.

Through the glass block window
fragile moonlight. Wind
in the bushes mutters curses.

Before I turn the lights off,
spider webs along the ceiling
whisper faint good nights.

Fall and Winter

Autumn Wantons

In fall the trees get naked
for a wild romp with the wind.
See the birches, ash, and oak trees
shiver, anticipating the fun.
Watch them then some
late September morn,
strip free their lithe
limbs waving in the storm.
Carefree and wanton,
scarce withdrawn,
they leave their blushes
scattered on the lawn.

Autumn Elegy

The wind-chimes cleave the air

       as late October winds

lash the evergreens,

       and green turns gold, then gray

in the fading afternoon.

Blood in the trees!

       blood in the trees!

Autumn is here and

       Marsyas is dead.

The Days Draw Back

The days draw back their warmth.
The night is full of separate stars.
The quiet like a conversation ended;
trees' leaves, scattered, letters never read.
The garden, empty after fruitful months,
the summer fire-pit a cold and empty place,
the burning bush, extinguished by a frost
that also chills the heart. A cream and striped
cat moves silently beneath the porch-side bush,
in search of little friends to play with in the night.

Peonies in Fall

In autumn, after the cold September rains
have browned their beds, the peonies
are left alone, leaves tarnished silver,
stalks now thin as spinsters' legs.
They hang over their metal rings
in tangles, seeking anyone to hold them up.

All fertile fullness gone, their seed pods—
shriveled vulvas of old maids—
hang exposed to cold October winds;
their fancy dresses from June a distant memory
of pink and white.

                    With bees
and other suitors gone, the flowerbed
becomes a home for ghosts and other haunts—
the summer's last cicadas hidden there,
and spiders in their tattered webs,
too cold to move beyond their vortices.

In Fall

In fall, along the highway slopes,
the sumac blooms. Rust cones—
like angry candles—flame
above the unexpected green
and ancient, vicious-looking leaves.
Clumps and sprays of fern-like foliage
create a canopy that shades
the lethal, sickle boughs.

Already ashen, amber-red,
the sumac whispers fall.
The bands of green and rust,
and cranberry, or black,
with bands of orange—
resemble berries of the mountain ash.

Rough cones, suspended
from the lurid branches
celebrate impending death.
Along the highway slopes,
the bare twigs pulse,
like branching veins;
fresh blood of autumn sacrifice.

Nature's Due

In Memory of Stanley Kunitz

Each morning, picking windfall Bartlett pears,
I find one chewed by something overnight.
The grass is wet and sticks to fruit I grasp
then cuddle to my chest to make a pile.
Thus burdened, I climb toward the house.
What came in the moist dark I can only guess.

I'm thankful, though, that it has gnawed just one,
leaving the rest for me to share with a grandchild
who loves pears. And so I climb the stairs,
arms embracing plump green-gold
that blesses the house with fragrance.
I know, as autumn skies grow dark:
with one gnawed gift from all that load of ripeness,
I have paid at least a part of nature's due.

A Bouquet

Crazy curls and semi-swirls
of spindly gray, thrust
from the grass,
the silver maple's
thin branches,
scattered on the lawn.
The boughs, the curlicues
and angles, bent which way
by wind and whim;
brittle and easy to break,
the smaller twigs snap;
they make a gray handful,
their twists and turns
the fate of living high
and falling low.

Crows

The crows,
like broken pieces
of the night,
dance out
above the roofs
and swirl
among the treetops
and the yards.

Late afternoon
and dingy blacktop
of a broken road,
lead me to think
of crows
as harbingers of fall.

Found Things

The sound of stone
    on metal;

        moon at mid-day
            in a pale blue sky.

The autumn cold
        invades the body
            like a warning,

  but the sun, the sun

        bestows a minor tone
            of warmth;
                a muted touch.

A last bee invades
        the foxglove's final,
            fragile bloom,
  hovers a moment;
        flies into oblivion.

Now, wait, attentive,
        for a sign of meaning
            in the coincidence

        of things experienced

  on an ordinary autumn day.

Parting Gifts

Fields of splintered light and broken glass;

    Diamond thoroughfares.

        sequined silver lawns;

            platinum patches, tinseled snail trails;

wispy foil, and threads of ice.

Crowds of cloud and rain and cold

    came through last night;

        departing winter's boisterous boys,

left scattered gifts; these gems, today.

Along the roads and in the fields

    delicate spires and webs of glass;

rare treasures, common riches everywhere.

Pendants from eaves; paths of pewter,

    tree branch, grass-stem, tendril,

        enameled with a coat of glass;

cords of chrysoprase.

The sun appears, and points of light

    that glitter in the glare,

        amaze the sight,

and here and there a touch of gold and red.

Widower Bald

A cold and snowy wind
blows through the pines
and hardwoods;

a view across the woods
and distant fields, obscured
by waves of sleet and snow.

Darkness falls, and clouds
fly tattered before the blast
of late March fury.

A male eagle broods
upon a nest of sticks
and feathers, dung, and bones.

With draggled wings and
yellow beak, the hooded
eyes stare through the night.

A mile away its mate
lies dead from causes
only God can know.

The nested eggs will never hatch;
the male may only
find another mate.

Is Nature's harsh,
exacting discipline
a lesson to our world?

Memories

Far From Home

Homage to Stanley Kunitz

We lived on a hill with far
too many rooms. The neighbors
spoke their oaken vows
the birds begat the sundown
and the morn. We moved
so often that the moon
forgot our names. The sisters
of the mysteries foretold their beads
while sooty welders wove
their webs of steel above
the mountains and below
the streams. On wheels
we wore our weary dreams
from East to West and back
the seasons ripening
beneath our feet. The empty
rooms abandoned what we
never meant to save.

My maiden aunts

composed on salvaged envelopes
cut open and laid flat to show
their pure insides (like fish
filleted by a letter opener);
a habit learned in the Depression
with the meager means that all endured.
For years they scavenged greeting cards
from which they cut the pictures
and the printed words to make
their patchwork palimpsests.
From a dozen cards might come
a single colored Christmas greeting
with a note, perhaps, handwritten on
the bottom or the back, to niece
or nephew who enjoyed the treat.

Walden, Colorado, 1953

A shanty, dragged in
from the range, stands,
hands in pockets,

beyond the last corral.
Outside, two urchins play
at cowboys in the sand.

Inside, their mother, left
to tend the hearth, is cooking
scrapple on a hot plate.

Dad returns from town
at dusk, driving back
to the ranch in a 1940 Ford.

A 1950s Memory

A&W Root Beer in a frosty glass, served
by a
carhop in orange skirt,
black top,
and saddle shoes.

A small town drive-in parking lot
beebop on the jukebox,
cacophony of teenage voices
blend the sounds
and sights.

A vision vivid as the taste of ice-cold root
beer, powerful as the smell of blacktop in the sun,
cloying as a teenage romance
brought back
acrid with the molten darkness of the past.

Ft. Collins, CO, 1953

In the fading light
of a double motel room
on New Year's Eve
my parents are carousing
with some friends.

The two-foot Christmas tree
with hand-made ornaments,
the Dixie cones with paint
and glitter, popcorn garland
strung, stands on a dresser
faded gray with age.

The men are drinking
boilermakers, telling stories
from the job; a three-week
tank repair. The women
hush them. "Don't
wake up the kids!"
Their voices fade.

Outside the Colorado winds
race down the front range
to the plains. The Poudre Valley
streams are frozen over now.

Last night, skating
in the darkness,
thrilling with the risk of
rocks or open water, we
recalled the meager Christmas
far away from any home
we'd known since school
let out last June;

a home on wheels
or any place besides
a cheap motel with
hotplate, pale-cream fridge
and nubbled coverlets.

In the night these memories
are fading as my breath
is fading on the window pane.
Yet I remain a last light
toward the fading darkness.
Am I home at last?

Polish Flat

From an upstairs window open
to the east, the glowing haze
of steel mills along Lake Michigan;
in the foreground a gray garage,
an alley, walk-ups, wire fences.

In the dark the children gaze,
the attic far too hot for sleep,
hot boxes of old clothes
and newsprint insulation;
mothballs slowly bleeding
into nothing in a cedar chest.

Parents and grandparents murmur
beneath them in Polish phrases
that they'll never understand.
They hear the squeaky rocking chair
as they lie there imagining
the tasseled lampshades
and cigar smoke on the air.

Sister, how little we knew
of ourselves and each other;
where we'd be in years ahead.

Paper Houses

As kids we built small houses
out of fours and nines and one-eyed jacks;
leaned colored rectangles
first side to side, then end to end;

then piled the stories on,
hoping to create a palace
or a tower; maybe just a
cottage or deserted hut.

Each pair of cards and roof card
seemed to give the structure
greater strength, make it stable
(never permanent).

So card would follow card
and even deck to deck,
small room and ante-room proliferate,
filling the entire tabletop.

Imagined people sheltered in
our afternoons of make-believe,
but every now and then

a house came crashing down,
entombing everyone in glossy ruins
of hearts and diamonds,
spades and clubs.

It's hard to lean one on another,
balance, gravity, or gentleness,
when all collapse at once
into a scattering of thins.

Like Faded Newspapers

Like faded and discarded newspapers,
the fragments of my past
blow up before my eyes.
I read without regret
the headlines, features
without nostalgia, pushing
always forward to tomorrow's
news, yet always fearful what
may lie ahead,
ignoring how the past
imprints the latest horror
that I plan.

Dancing in Time

Homage to Ilya Kaminsky

We lived west of the past
the mountains sent us letters
we couldn't read.

Grandparents a country away
boiled weenies in the attic
aunts pulled rosaries and cigars
from house-dresses, babushkas
and hung up enema bags.

I wore a coonskin cap
that understood my loneliness
hid in my smiles
and in my sister's drawers
like a prairie dog.

Winter on the plains
stripped us bare
(I feared its teeth)
my mother longed
for a home with more
and less than wheels
or cows to milk or steal. At this my father

rubbed his bald head
blinked his sunburnt
eyes and went out to shoot
his .22 at rats and
naked dime store manikins.

The truth of this is
in the hearing.
Do you hear?

Out of Africa and Places Near and Far

Africa

Malawi 1969

Clay-colored floors and baseboards,
swept by a Bantu male in livery;
a British guest-house bar on the road
between Blantyre and Dedza,
on the dusty Lilongwe Road.

The wine is Portuguese, the conversation
racist, the accent Afrikaans.
The volunteers are silent guests
in this the newly independent Africa.

"Kaffirs! Can't trust one,"
the bearded man in khaki shorts
and shirt intones, hairs on his arms
as red as brush haircut and facial hair.
Red-faced, he orders whisky, grabs his crotch,
then tells a dirty joke, hoping to get
the female Peace Corps volunteers to blush.

Hotel Malawi

Homage to Charles Simic

I liked my digs, a window on the jungle.
At dusk, the monkeys stared at me.
Outside, the villagers walked
down the clay path, through the dambo
to the tea plantation. A crippled woman
carried a suitcase on her head.

Mostly, though, I sought the quiet after dark;
the rooms, with spiders, fleas and roaches
that wore brown jackets, underneath the iron bed;
the geckos dreaming on the walls; a night so black
I scarcely looked outside, lest horrors
meet me in the windows' mirror.

At 5 A.M. the voices in the dawn,
the bare feet soughing in the dark—
imagined women, Dar-cloth skirts,
baskets on their heads. Going to the john—
another night of native beer—I heard
a baby's cry; pictured it tightly wrapped
on mother's back, and thought
I heard a months old homesick cry.

Chikale Beach

Malawi, Central Africa, 1969

Down to the bay
in the gathering dusk,
then out through town.
Beyond the DC's house
and shadows loom ahead.

The bridge across the dambo,
rotted, scarce will hold
the load of motorcycle,
man—and woman
clinging to his back,
like a cricket
to its mate.

Uphill and then
a dusty, steep
descent into the crowd
that gathers at the beach.

On the sloping sand
they've lit a fire.
There they dance,
drink Carlsberg beer
or Malawi Gin and lime
until the morning haze
arises like an Ngoni warrior.

Then they mount their rides
again, escape through jungle
towards a sunrise over Africa.

Cinzano White, and Red

A gaudy restaurant poster for vermouth;
the grapes, the swirls of color, edged
in black, around a supine model
whose flying hair obscures her face.

The flavor of the sight is sweet, astringent,
with just a hint of wormwood;
passion over ice, enjoyed
before and after meals
or sex.

Years ago, it was a favorite
drink in Central Africa.

Pungent midnight, the southern stars so near;
ex-pat passengers, female and male;
lovers and friends on the open upper deck;
a packet, anchored in the bay.

Faint lights from the shore, reflected on the water,
mix with the stars. Below,
the sounds of Bantu passengers
embarking noisily; the thrumming
of the diesel, surging, surging to push off.

Now the present takes possession
of the past again. But the past
refuses to dissolve.

A ship sets out for Mozambique, the north;
a steamy Greene adventure, freighted
with passion and regrets.

So now, a farewell sip,
a final toast. You ghosts
of yesteryear, adieu.
Return, remain; so far
away, so near, so dear.

Farewell to Africa

Chaka Zulu screwed his mother
in the road outside our house.
The smaller dog had been in heat
a week before her son, a big
black village dog mounted her
as Tim and I walked home
one morning after class. My roommate
and I watched as we argued, drank
our morning chicory:
fraternal rivalry in Africa.
The houseboy brought us scones with butter.
Zulu went at it even after Tim and I
went back our separate ways
to class. When he was done,
Zulu and Sally stayed connected till
we two came back for lunch.

The weeks flew by. The school
put on a celebration: farewell to our volunteer.
With dancing, drums, and Land Rovers
of guests, we bid goodbye to Tim,
enroute to Canada.

Weeks later Sally gave birth
beneath my roommate's empty
iron bed. Our houseboy drowned
the litter in the dambo after dark;
cleaned up the mess was left behind.

The Neighborhood

Rummage Sale

An ordinary August Saturday. Then,
in the neighborhood, a kind of magic;
old faces stare from older picture frames;
sterling silver, plant arrangements, canning jars;

an antique lamp, old books,
a box of dated record albums,
painted birdhouses, a baize card table, dishes,
make-up mirrors, a German choir book.

The visitors drawn slowly up the driveway
in the sun, threading the narrow aisles,
stop to peer at hand-sewn toys, or turn
a porcelain elephant in their hands.

Swept into the dark garage itself,
in rusty light, damp carpet
beneath low rafters, here they try
on funny glasses by the light of a dirty bulb.

Past chipped, enameled pans and faux
Depression glass, to Rosie, eighty years old,
lurking behind the tables in an easy
chair, the darkest corner of the room.

A spider in her web, she weaves her words;
the past hangs in her hair like dust. Outside
the sun shines off the asphalt drive, and buyers,
blinded, emerge with cobwebs in their heads.

Before Midnight

The dark street stands deserted.
Only the home, emptied
by divorce, with one dim bulb,

glows weakly, like a dying body.
Its cone of light surveys the yard—
a garden overgrown and haunted

by ghosts of parties past;
a phantom swimming pool
where only shadows float.

The shrouded moon emerges,
an aged Charon counting
small change into a trembling hand.

Suburban Derelict

A cluttered porch, forgotten
and unvisited, its awning coated
by neglect, the badly painted door a ruin.

The eaves drip desolation,
the sidewalk strewn with leaves
of loss. The driveway cratered

by the cares of decades. Flowerbeds
are weed-choked with forgetfulness.
The empty mailbox gapes decrepitude.

Around the corner, more suburban slums;
a sign "For Rent" obscured by buckthorn, toys
abandoned on the street, a kite upended in a tree.

35th & Morgan

A house atop a hill,
garage door half collapsed,
a slanted porch above;
in front an unkempt lawn.

The duplex window shades
pulled down unevenly,
the front door open wide
this cold November morning.

To see straight through the hall
into a living room
and dining room feels
almost obscene—

a woman, legs spread wide,
and lying on her back.

Tam's Gone Dark

Snow lies deep in the parking lot
of the Chinese restaurant. Closed.
Abandoned? No deliveries? No
late-night carry-outs, with soy
sauce in the little plastic bags?
No Egg foo Yung? The sign,
"Chop Suey," hangs at an angle,
as it had for years before
this sudden end. No boiling
oil in woks? no paper hats,
black aprons, or black slippers
on the help? The Chinese lanterns
above the door are dark; two snow-white
plaster lions crouch beside the entrance,
guarding the place from no one, now.

Up North, Out West

Silos

Almost hidden in the trees
the gray shapes loom
behind abandoned farms,
silent monuments of past
prosperity or ruin,
markers of a nation's
monumental disregard.

They're mostly empty now
of the fear and dread
and hopelessness that
grew too large to be
contained, or harvested;
except for rats
and bats, and birds
lost in their darker
heights and depths.

Talmadge River Brown

Remembering Ted Hughes

Dark trout move, unseen, in pools
below the curl of water from the dam.
Scotch pines, dark and stiff, move with a chill
Superior wind that breaks the evening calm.
I hear the plunge and pop of fish that rise
to take mosquitoes from the air. The sound, absorbed,
becomes a part of water moving in and out of the pond
on its rocky way from Iron Range to lake.

After dusk we sit and shine a light across the pond,
where smells of water—iron tinctured—and white pine unite.
The stream runs clear. Trout plunge at insects circling up
from the dark surface. Small fish make silver pocks.
Twelve-inch stock fish shatter the surface
with the hopeless wrench of homeless tramps.
A shiny roll means larger fish that swallow
their prey, then disappear into the depths.

Only now and then a monster brown arises
to break the glassy shield repeatedly—
each gulp almost inaudible among the sounds of summer night.
It feeds in regal silence, then leaves the teeming surface world,
and the sub-surface realm of gliding shadows,
to sound again the dark crevices of rock, beside tree roots,
near icy, pre-Cambrian springs.

The Talmadge River empties into Lake Superior on Minnesota's north shore.

At Dillman's

Early, early morning darkness,
quiet at the resort. Thunder
in the distance, coming closer
with the dawn.
Suddenly, a thousand whispers,
rain on roofs and through the white
pines, down to the point,
then out across the lake.

Lights on in the main lodge,
smaller lights in Little Denmark,
Golden Pond; reflections
in the asphalt drives,
the playground wet
and quiet as another day begins.

Then, later, when artistic work
is done, participants relaxing
in Adirondack chairs,
or around their fire rings.

Dillman's is a famous artists' retreat in northern Wisconsin.

In the Driftless

Homage to Ben Logan

The watercress stays green all winter in the valley springs.
Along the ridges prehistoric cliffs and around more recent
mounds the birch and alder grow. The railroad ran through here
a dozen decades in the past, through tunnels, over bridges,
carrying grain and cattle, passengers and crews.

Now the fog hangs heavy over sand mines, machinery
dealerships and fewer farms. The streams still flow and trout
still swim, but now the storied past is less than dream.

The hill country was full of voices when horses pulled the plows
and women churned butter in the shade of milking sheds.

Out here a year is an arbitrary thing, unlike the changes
of the moon the coming of the snow, the coming of the spring.

The 'Driftless" is an unglaciated portion of the American Midwest that
encompasses portions of four states: Wisconsin, Illinois, Iowa, and Minnesota.

Davenport, IA

Haunted by train whistles
and black iron,
since those first
three engines back in 1856,
I dream of trestles,
tunnels and the bridges
crossing mighty waters.

Levees, lowlands,
farmers sliding
down the slopes
from cornfields
to the river.

Davenport, backwater
to the Midwest,
where casinos
sprawl on riverboats,

and debutants prance
down the halls of largely
empty downtown night spots,
nostalgic for the past.

Gill's Rock

Icy water boils
around the stones
and pebbles
on this northern shore.

The winds from Michigan
blow cold and raw
as whitecaps race
from east to west.

Across the narrow strait
the island named
for our first president
holds steady in the gale;

ironic icon, feeble sign
of hope indicting a faithless world.

Gill's Rock is the northern-most settlement on Wisconsin's Door Peninsula. It
looks out on Washington Island, which lies a few miles to the northwest.

Pilgrimage

Distant, almost unreachable,
the Cana Island Lighthouse,
visible above the evergreens
far out into the lake, stands
inaccessible. The stony shore,
its worn and rounded limestone
shaped like speckled eggs or broken
bones, the twisted roots of spruce
that grip the shore, the winding road
that leaves you distant from the lighthouse
yet; from a spit of sand, across the nearby
bay, the Cana Island Lighthouse
rises still calm, serene, and unassailable.

The Cana Island Lighthouse is a landmark and tourist destination on the Lake
Michigan side of the Door County peninsula in northeastern Wisconsin.

Washington Island Tale

For Christie

White stones shape
the cove where ferries
dock, load up with tourists
and head out again
for Detroit Bay.

Blue above blue water
the deep contrast of land
and lake and sky.

Above the shore
in shadows of the pines
the Northport
Tourist Information Center
stands, commanding
the beach, protecting cars
left in the woods by island dwellers.

Princess of the Center,
she greets, makes small talk
answers questions with a smile
and shares her knowledge
of the past and present Door.

The daughter of an island family,
she grew up watching water,
teaching school, then tended
bar at Karly's. Now she helps
the visitors from far away
with gossip, island lore,
suggestions what to see.

Met a ferry captain
who liked this island girl.
They married on a ferry;
the passengers began to worry
at the appointed time, when the boat
dropped anchor short of port;
they called the Coast Guard.
It was just the ceremony
taking place; the vows
exchanged between
the island and the mainland
between the sailor and the maid.

Far & Farewell

At an Exhibition

A shapely blonde—in partial profile, sleeveless
black shell, patterned skirt—looks sidelong
at a life-size Art Nouveau, an odalisque
in striking black and white, who, like a wanton,
breasts and cleft exposed, long legs
extended leisurely, against a *Judgendstil*
background, reclines; a Klimt-inspired robe
snaking about her curves. She lounges
on a pillow, face shaped by short hair
that frames an eyeless space, the lips and nipples
poised expressive of a cool eroticism.

A Gift from France

for Suzie & Rick

Unlike an ordinary cup,
my mug from St. Michel
sounds different when I
stir it with a shiny spoon.

I think of fair Limoges,
the fragile clay:
a hollow sound, a bit like
hammered tin, a water bucket
or a scuttle for the coal
outside a store
that one might find in
any village near the
sea-surrounded church.

I stir the mug again,
its rim and handle so unearthly blue.
The tea is sweet and gently brown,
like late-spring water in a French canal.

I see the church atop its mount;
the flock of birds, the boat;
the ocean—blue, but flecked
with clouds—and rest
in silent gratitude.

Remembering Fountains

for Karen Zealand, 1999

You came so far and never saw
beyond your navel.

You transformed transcendent intimations
into self-centered fears.

The quiet of the cloister stones
was too much for you.
Instead of vaulting love
and choirs

you chose to think of
pain and loss,
and sex.

Locked in a *fin de siècle* mindset,
you never heard
these myriad stones, so many monks,
so many centuries of song.

Remembered into life by language,
you and I can only hope to leave
memorials like theirs,
but only if we lose ourselves as they did,
rather than defame
their ruins.

"Fountains" is another name for the ruined abbey of Rievaulx, in northern
England. This poem was inspired by Karen Zealand's "Rievaulx."

Vacancy

A sign, "FOR RENT,"
half-hidden by the trees,
captures the imagination
of a child once homeless,
hopeless, friendless in
the western wilderness;
the memory of motels
flats and mobile homes
to rent and once
a haunted house.

This house behind the trees
seems shaded by despair
shadowed by the stories
of those who left with rent
unpaid and boxes of baby things
piled high against the back wall
of a dark garage whose
recesses hide the secrets
of successive lodgers
gone without a clue.

From the Air

Above the plane, immensity;
below, a winter desert,
lit in places.
Millions sleep beneath
the billions of cold lights—

like snowflakes
frozen in a void—while one,
a sleepless father
turns on a porch light
for an errant daughter,
drawn by phantom novas
from the bright way
leading home.

Moments Strange

Line in the Wind

The lusty spring wind
blows the laundry,
pulling the clothes-line
taut as a bowstring.
Sailing out, but not
like arrows, the man's
jeans dance with the gale,
while, holding on by just
one pin, a woman's
panties, nearly off,
try to whip
modestly behind.

Thief of the Night

The warm September night is loud
with crickets. Clouds are fading
in the night sky; street lights fairly
shout their light across the lawn
and through the garden, ghost-shadows
behind the trees. The evergreens eat
shadows; the flagpole stands, a silent
witness to the night, its other sounds
and visitors.
              Before I sleep I'll close
the blinds, the shades, the curtains,
fearful what might happen out of doors.
The floor will groan, the fridge will throw
a fit, and lights from cars will shudder
from the ceiling, waken me
at 1 a.m., to face my demons, herd
the heartaches like a flock of sheep.
The notebook, poised to catch my dreams,
lies still, inert, its pages curled like lips
that will not speak. The pillows, blankets,
waiting to smother me, are silent, patient.

Hours pass. I pray, I count, I try
my yoga breathing; nothing helps. I'm
beached, a fish with gills extended, red
and jagged, reaching for the water: sleep,
an element in which to lose the sense
of time, the sense of self, the shelf
of life on which we stand, tiptoe, about to
fall—or leap. About to leave, and, leaving,
know not what one leaves, but knowing
nothing less than everything that's real.

The bed is hard, but warm milk heated, stirred,
then swallowed before the long wait for dawn
is thoughtlessly forgotten as sleep comes
like a thief, to rob me of my fears.

Waking in a Fog

Asleep, then half-asleep;
awake, disoriented,
groping, grasping
sheets, then air,
I rise, open the shade
then see therein
my self, reflected
in the opaque pane.

Outside the fog hangs
heavy on the trees,
between the houses,
rising from the grass.

Inside, dark thoughts
and shadowy desires
swirl up from moist
dreams that turn
to cream then leave
to make the day.

Along the sidewalk
ghosts who wear their hoodies
haunt the neighborhood,
faces all but black, opaque
beneath, within the dream
that is a foggy day.

At the Heart Clinic

An aged woman's leathery face,
the short jaw set and resolute;
determined to survive. Short blonde
hair, combed like a man's; her jeans
and checked blue shirt also bely her gender.
She sits and stares; she tears a page
from a tabloid magazine and folds it;
tucks it carefully in her shirt.

A longish wait. She works her jaw,
her hawk's eyes sweep the room.
Suddenly, the face, a ghost
out of the past. I look
in people's faces,
find my long dead there.

Out of Season

In mid-July the house—a washed-out beige,
set back a distance from the road—displays
a dingy Christmas wreath on its front door.
Three ragged trees spread pale-green leaves
over the roof on which a sun-bleached
Santa Claus tips perilously close
to the gutter with its disconnected
downspout. A gravel driveway, empty,
rutted, leads around the house to darkness
at midday. The heat, oppressive, hints
of mysteries no burning Yule reveals.

The Moon a Burlesque Artist

The moon, a burlesque artist,
teases us. A flimsy veil
covers her face.

A moment later,
there she is,
revealed, a naked queen;

so cool, so distant—
glowing though—
and coming

full;
her ripeness
palpable.

What would we *do*
without our sister moon,
who teaches, both voluptuous
and coy?

Blood Moon

November 30, 2017

The blood moon rises, as the crickets
trill, and children shout in darkness
down the block. The night is ostentatious
with events. The pope has left the country
to its evil and its sin, having offered
forgiveness, joy, and hope to the many
who have followed him.

               Now the moon becomes
less bright as our earth passes between it
and the sun. The children's shouts increase;
eclipse has loosed a strange contagion,
giddiness, upon the world.

               It happens slowly,
this eclipse of blood.
A shadow crosses, blotting out the faces
the moon has made at us all summer.
Now September fogs and frosts have passed,
and now the moon is passing too. Will it
return? Or will we be left to find
our way and our love in darkness
after the moon has set?

Black Icarus

A poor man drops
from the sky; falls into
Clapham;
food and clothes left
in the gear-well
of the BOAC flight
from Africa.

Who persuaded him that
he could live and breathe
at forty-thousand feet
for half a day aloft?

What myth that promised
wealth or freedom drove
him to ignore the facts of flight?

White Rabbit

Woodstock, NY, 1969

"White Rabbit" runs through all my dreams,
chased by an airplane, flown by a luscious witch
whose tossing tassels tease her tits. She's all in white,
her voice is silky smoke and gravel and her feet
are bare. I still imagine I was there. She slinks
across the stage, the microphone erect and at
her open mouth. "One pill!" she shouts and I
am ready to swallow anything she might give.

Woman Alone

Hinckley, MN, 2019

What is she doing here
on a bench outside
a cheap motel at dawn?

The sky is overcast and black.

Knit cap t-shirt
ear-buds and sweater
hoodie backpack
wool socks pulled up
over faded jeans
and well-worn Ugg-boots.

Horizon dark with snow.

Leans elbows
on her knees
a cord hanging down.

The clouds lie close; horizon disappears;

look in a face
no longer young
dusty brown hair
a few stray strands
beside the face.

The clouds drive east before October winds.

Not sadness, perhaps
Resignation, stoic
perseverance
in that empty
stare. For whom, or why
is she waiting there?

Looking for Norma

After decades, I've been looking for you, Norma,
in the basement of my heart. The light from boarded windows, bad,
the lamps without their bulbs.

The furnace now is old, the plumbing on the verge.
The empty bar is dry, the table tennis table piled
with junk and extra mattresses. Absurd!

I moved the boxes, caught in cobwebs, re-arranged
the toys. I opened musty trunks of memories. I felt
the pulse of days forgotten; found a battered dress,

some yellow underwear; old hats and model airplanes.
Pictures in old frames stare back at me. I read
the books and poems you gave me,
tried on clothes that you once wore.

I lay upon the broken couch, its springs poked
through my back. Beneath the workbench, dust
and mouse turds stopped my search.
I crawled back up the stairs and poured a drink
before I called the hearse.

Found at Last

Under the gray stone bridge
where the whirlpool licks
debris left after the winter
thaw and spring rains,
amid the tangled
tree limbs, tires, and twisted
junk she rests at last,
as from a journey.
Little enough remains. The trip
downriver took its toll.
She'd stop occasionally,
pause and whirl, but current
pressing matters bore her
on to where it all would end.

Aubade

Flies breeding in the dusty room,
the clothing in the closet hangs
in shreds. The body on the bed
is decades dead. The woman
next to him ignores the flies.
She strokes the painted poodle
in her arms and stares at cracks
that mark the ceiling, singing notes
that make no sense.

When the sun comes up the moths
are lost and now appear a hundred ways
to woe. The land invades the sky
and mind knows nothing. Everyone
refuses lemons beneath the summer sun.
All must devour husks as, when
the sun comes up with single stinking
eye, the burning sand
*   laughs underneath the feet.*

Summer Evening

It's sunset, and the scouts
are out, shouting
in the yard next door.
Male voices of uncertain age
cry" 'Caught it."
Metal bat hits leather ball.
To taste the zest, the sweat
and freedom of the night.
Their changing voices bark.

Now they're playing in the dark.
The voices, louder—almost ghostly—
echo far across the field.
A dried up cricket crawls
along the sidewalk, scrapes
its elbows, goes looking
for an empty grave.

Now louder shouts disturb
the air and streak again
the moonless indigo with raw
vehement, almost vulpine cries.

By the Lake

The box kite bobs and jerks
five hundred feet
above the shoreline park,
the string, like fish line
with a lunker on.

Bucking, swinging side
to side, the kite is diving, darting
like a thing possessed.

To pull the string with fingers
might draw blood.
The wind is strong,
the kite fights any effort
to bring it down.
Taut between earth and sky
it pulls the mind into a world
of forces immemorial.

About the Author

Born in Manitowoc, Wisconsin, Ed Block traveled with his family throughout the West during his youth. After high school and college in St. Paul, Minnesota, he served in the Peace Corps in Malawi, Central Africa, before earning his Ph.D. in English and comparative literature from Stanford University. He is now Emeritus Professor of English at Marquette University, Milwaukee, WI, where, until his retirement in 2012, he taught a variety of literature courses, concluding his career with capstone courses on Denise Levertov and Czeslaw Milosz and workshops in creative writing. A gardener and birdwatcher for decades, he has found inspiration in the ordinary and the extraordinary; the mundane and the strange.

His poems have appeared in *Plainsongs, Nebraska Life, Lake Country Journal, Museletter, CrossCurrents,* and a variety of other venues. Besides publishing or editing books and numerous literary articles, he is the author of three poetry collections: *Anno Domini* (2016), *Seasons of Change* (2017) and *Shell Dreams* (2021). His interviews, essays, and reviews on literary topics, have appeared in a variety of journals. He continues to write poetry, tend a garden, and enjoy retirement in Greendale, Wisconsin.

www.ingramcontent.com/pod-product-compliance
Lightning Source LLC
Chambersburg PA
CBHW070502090426
42735CB00012B/2659